Original title:
Life: You Can't Always Find the Meaning

Copyright © 2025 Creative Arts Management OÜ
All rights reserved.

Author: Charles Whitfield
ISBN HARDBACK: 978-1-80566-290-7
ISBN PAPERBACK: 978-1-80566-585-4

The Search for Fleeting Truths

I wandered through a circus tent,
Chasing shadows, where time is spent.
A juggler smiled with a wink,
He said, "Did you stop to think?"

The clowns all danced in silly shoes,
With painted frowns and joyous blues.
A fortune teller brewed her tea,
"The answer's just not meant for thee!"

In the Labyrinth of Uncertainty

I took a stroll through twisty lanes,
Where every turn brought silly pains.
A minotaur with a goofy hat,
Asked, "Have you seen my missing cat?"

Each corner echoed random shouts,
As I searched for the way out.
A signpost read, "Nowhere near!"
With a grin, I faced my fear.

A Journey Beyond the Light

I journeyed far past shining stars,
To find the truth, or so I thought.
A comet zoomed with a cheeky grin,
"The answers aren't found where you've sought!"

Chasing fireflies in the dark,
I laughed at every little spark.
"They're just here for the fun, my friend!"
A witty joke that had no end.

Echoes of Forgotten Paths

In woods where echoes twist and tease,
I searched for wisdom on the breeze.
The trees were giggling, leaves a-chatter,
"What are you seeking? It don't matter!"

A rabbit with a watch was late,
Said, "Stop and smell the garden plate!"
With every step, I lost the track,
The hidden truth? I turned my back.

Beyond the Horizon of Thought

I searched for wisdom, high and low,
But all I found was a funky old toe.
It wiggled and jiggled, calling me near,
I chuckled and thought, 'This can't be it, dear!'

An owl in a bow tie named Fred gave tips,
On dancing with shadows and doing cool flips.
He blinked with both eyes—what a curious sight,
And said, 'Just enjoy, it's all quite all right!'

The Clarity of Chaos

A blender whirred in my head today,
Mixing my thoughts in a zany bouquet.
I peeked inside—what a colorful mess,
Maybe confusion is just a form of finesse?

The cat wore a hat and danced on the wall,
While socks in the dryer had a wild ball.
Amidst all the nonsense, a giggle was found,
Perhaps in the madness, joy can abound!

Sifting Through the Sands of Doubt

On a beach of confusion, I tried to collect,
Golden grains of truth, what did I expect?
But seagulls swooped down, causing a ruckus,
They squawked, 'Just make castles, don't fuss with the fuss!'

I built a tall tower, but it tumbled right down,
As crabs formed a union, clacking their crowns.
With laughter I joined, living in play,
Who needs deep meaning, when you can just sway?

The Art of Embracing Uncertainty

They say life's a puzzle, all bits and all pieces,
But mine's more like cheese where uncertainty ceases.
I sliced it and diced it, made quite a plate,
Only to find out it's starting to date!

With each funky fork, I took a wild dive,
Navigating flavors, my taste buds alive.
In unpredictability, I found a delight,
For laughter and chaos make everything bright!

The Secret Garden of Forgotten Dreams

In a garden where weeds thrive,
Old dreams dance, trying to survive.
They trip on roots of stubborn thoughts,
While squirrels laugh at all they've sought.

Gnomes wear hats that seem too tight,
Whisper secrets in the night.
A butterfly flits, with zero care,
Saying, "What's the point? Here, we share!"

Beehives buzz with plans askew,
While flowers bloom in shades askew.
The sun peeks through with a grin wide,
Is joy found in each bumpy ride?

Patterns in the Unplanned

Chaos reigns in the quilt we sew,
Stitching life without a show.
Random patches of laughter, tears,
Each square echoes quirky fears.

The cat naps on the blueprint's map,
It's upside down—oh, what a trap!
Patterns emerge in a strange dance,
That make us chuckle at fate's chance.

Unexpected rainbows paint the sky,
While clouds complain with a sulky sigh.
The weatherman shrugs, takes a break,
"Let's see what chaos we can make!"

The Riddle of the Unseen

Behind closed doors, a riddle hides,
Where socks disappear, and truth subsides.
The fridge hums wise philosophical tunes,
While leftovers plot under silver spoons.

A goldfish knows the meaning of glee,
While pondering what it means to be.
Its bowl, a world that's oh so small,
Yet even fish can sometimes feel tall.

Invisible ink on the heart's great scroll,
We scribble doodles but lose control.
In every laugh, a secret breathes,
Caught in the webs our own mind weaves.

Embers in the Darkness

In the night, the embers spark,
Revealing whispers in the dark.
They crackle joyfully and tease,
While shadows dance around like cheese!

Lost socks haunt the quiet space,
A mystery more than a silly race.
With pizza crumbles in hand they flirt,
As if they know how to exert.

A dreamer stumbles on cobwebbed thought,
Where wisdom's forged in what's been sought.
Yet here we sit, with laughter's glow,
Finding warmth in what we don't know.

The Hidden Threads of Existence

In the cupboard, socks go missing,
Cereal dances, on mornings unblissing.
The old cat stares at the wall, quite wise,
While I fumble through life, seeking the prize.

Why do we ponder on things so complex?
When the fridge hums soft like a guilty text.
Chasing rainbows with shoes untied,
Fumbling like clowns, in this chaotic ride.

Dancing in the Dark

Under the moon, I trip on my shoe,
Falling like metronomes—oh, who knew?
Laughter erupts with every clumsy twist,
As shadows join in, they can't be dismissed.

A tango with dust bunnies, quite the sight,
Eating leftover pizza, heartily at night.
Spinning around, without a clear plan,
Just me and my thoughts, in this glorious jam.

Beneath the Surface of What's Seen

Look closer, there's chaos beneath the calm,
Like fish wearing hats, a peculiar charm.
The mailman arrives with bills and with glee,
Unknowingly adding to life's mystery.

The dog thinks he's a mighty lion's pride,
While reality keeps him tethered and tied.
In the garden, weeds bloom like fond memories,
A riddle wrapped up in dark breezy trees.

The Map of Wandering Souls

A map drawn in crayon, no streets to be found,
I wander like a goose, all lost and unwound.
The stars giggle softly, unsure what to say,
As I trip over thoughts about yesterday.

I sketched my journey on a napkin so bold,
But the ink leaks out, like secrets untold.
With each step I take, more laughter appears,
As I dance with confusion, and embrace all the cheers.

The Art of Wandering

I wandered off to find my peace,
But ended up in quite the crease.
The ducks all stared, the grass looked mad,
And all I wanted was a snack, how bad.

I asked a tree for some advice,
It just stood there, wasn't very nice.
Like trying to read a menu in the dark,
Got lost again, what a lark!

The clouds were gossiping up so high,
While squirrels plotted, oh me, oh my.
I tripped on words that weren't even said,
Who knew confusion could fill my head?

So here I am, with snacks in tow,
Finding meaning is a massive no.
Instead, I'll laugh and skip and hum,
Just wandering where all the funny's from.

Chasing Wisps of the Unseen

I chased a thought that slipped away,
Like glitter on a windy day.
It sparkled bright, then plopped and fizzed,
What was that? Oh well, I whizzed!

The shadows winked as I walked by,
They whispered secrets, oh so sly.
But every time I leaned in close,
They giggled hard, those sneaky ghosts!

I climbed a hill and saw a dream,
It waved hello, then lost its gleam.
With every step, I slipped and slid,
Who knew wisdom was a playful kid?

So here I go, on paths unseen,
Laughing with thoughts that float like cream.
If meaning hides like a shy raccoon,
I'll dance in circles—why not, it's June!

Shadows of a Silent Compass

My compass spun in dizzy cheer,
It pointed left then right, oh dear!
It said to go the straightest path,
But laughed so loud, I felt its wrath.

The sunlight played peek-a-boo,
Like it had a secret, just a few.
I chased my shadow, but it took flight,
Oh, how it giggled deep in night!

I asked the wind where I should roam,
It whirled and hurled, said, 'Find a home!'
But not a single clue it gave,
Just tickled me like it was brave!

So off I trot with silly glee,
Embracing all the mystery.
If meaning's hiding in plain sight,
I'll just keep laughing, feeling light!

The Unseen Narrative

Once upon a time, it seems,
I followed threads of hopeful dreams.
Yet every plot twist felt absurd,
Like talking to a flightless bird.

The pages fluttered, smiles in tow,
Each chapter turned to let me know.
That meaning's not a straight-lined quest,
Instead, it's just a funny jest!

A dog barked out a heartfelt truth,
While children giggled, bright in youth.
The world's a storybook with a twist,
And I'm the author of the missed!

So here's to tales that bend and sway,
Leaping into the light of day.
If unseen plots are all that gleam,
I'll write in laughter, chase each dream!

The Path of Questioning

Why do I trip on every stone?
Is it the path or just my clone?
Questions bounce like a rubber ball,
Answers vanish, I stumble, I fall.

Pondering over yesterday's toast,
Was that a ghost or just a boast?
Every riddle pulled from my shoe,
Perhaps the answer is just too blue.

Between Silence and Sound

The cat meows, a deep debate,
Did it just eat, or meditate?
Whispers float on the breeze so light,
Like thoughts that slip away from sight.

My phone buzzes with texts unmade,
Is it my friend, or just a charade?
Between the silence and the noise,
I choose to dance with my lost toys.

The Enigma of Unfulfilled Desires

I chased a donut, bright and sweet,
Only to find a rogue beat sheet.
The more I yearn, the farther it goes,
Like trying to sniff a garden hose.

A wish on a star that missed its flight,
Does it know it's lost or feels alright?
With every longing, a laugh ensues,
The universe plays with quirky clues.

The Dance of Impermanence

A sock disappears, a sock appears,
Is this a dance of fabric fears?
Round and round, they spin with glee,
While I just question, "Where's my key?"

Life's a party, but who's the host?
We raise our glasses, but here's the most:
The punchline comes, we all will sway,
Yet ponder where we'll end up, hey!

Riddles of the Heart

Why does my toaster toast a shade?

Is love a game that's poorly played?

Cornered by socks without a mate,

I ponder still, is this my fate?

Jellybeans dance, they make me grin,

While mysteries frolic deep within.

I ask the moon for a clever hint,

But it just laughs, and doesn't print.

In Search of the Unknown

I've lost my keys, oh dear, oh me!

They vanish like my cup of tea.

Searching the couch for clues untold,

Where treasures hide and tales unfold.

Questions about the cat's intent,

Why's it staring with such contempt?

Philosophers claim the cat's aloof,

But I just want to find the proof.

The Fragility of Understanding

Why do my plants seem quite so frail?
They only bring me tales of wails.
Try talking soft, I feed them light,
But they just wilt by following night.

Grappling thoughts like jarred jam,
I reach for meanings, but what a scam!
Words tumble out like candy corn,
Sticky and sweet, yet oddly worn.

Maps Without Directions

I bought a map, but it's a ruse,

The X was placed in the wrong shoes.

Wandering paths that lead to fun,

But none of them point at the sun.

Compass spins like a top on speed,

Who knew that happiness was a need?

Getting lost feels like a game,

Yet all the roads feel much the same.

Driftwood in an Endless Stream

A piece of wood just floats along,
It doesn't care where it belongs.
Swaying right and swaying left,
Joined by currents, it's quite bereft.

It dodges branches, dodges stones,
Whispering secrets in funny tones.
With every twist and turn it takes,
It chuckles at the mess it makes.

A splash! A laugh! Oh what a sight,
A surfboard under the moonlight.
Who knew driftwood could be so spry?
It rides the waves and wonders why.

Embracing waves, it finds its fun,
An endless trip, no need to run.
Through murmurs soft and laughs so loud,
Just floating by, it's feeling proud.

Fleeting Glimpses of Clarity

In shadows deep, a thought appears,
Like socks that vanish, fraught with fears.
A wink of sense, a puff of smoke,
Just when you think, it's a silly joke.

Sitting still, you suddenly see,
A spark of wisdom, whoopee!
But just as fast, it flies away,
Like breakfast toast on a new day.

Chasing thoughts that slip your mind,
A riddle wrapped in jokes, you'll find.
You laugh because you know it's true,
Clarity's just a prankster too.

So grab a joke and hold it tight,
Enjoy the whimsical delight.
For clarity's a fleeting guest,
In jest and jive, we find our rest.

Beyond the Veil of Certainty

Behind the curtain, secrets hide,
Like a cat who takes a funky ride.
You think you know, then off it darts,
With every twist, it steals your hearts.

Logic's cloak, a splendid guise,
Yet underneath, a clownish surprise.
You reach for truth, it plays a prank,
It laughs so hard, then floats and sank.

In riddles spun with eager cheer,
The answers dance but disappear.
A circus act without a ring,
Just grab your hat and let it swing.

So take your doubts and flip them round,
Embrace the circus, laughter's sound.
Lost in confusion, but oh so bright,
In the dark, we find our light.

Mosaic of Misunderstandings

Each piece is different, a jigsaw mix,
Thoughts twist and turn like silly tricks.
With colors bright that clash and play,
In this art, we find our way.

A puzzled face, a laughter shared,
When meanings twist and none are spared.
We bumble through with winks and nods,
In this chaos, we find the gods.

From blunders bold to giggles sweet,
This crazy dance cannot be beat.
With every slip, a new refrain,
In misunderstandings, we find our gain.

So grab a piece and place it right,
In this fun mess, we take delight.
For in the puzzle, laughter's key,
Misunderstood, yet wild and free.

The Complexity of Simplicity

A cat on a roof, chasing its tail,
With conquering dreams, yet destined to fail.
The sun in the sky, so bright and so clear,
Soldiers of socks march into the drear.

With pancakes for breakfast and cereal fights,
We juggle our hopes on wild, sleepless nights.
The spoon's got a twist, the fork's in a bind,
A dance of the kitchen — oh, how we unwind.

The carpet's a sea, we're pirates on quests,
Exploring the corners, avoiding all tests.
Each glance in the mirror, who's winning this race?
The eyebrows are marching, oh what a face!

Our hearts beat to rhythms of puzzled delight,
As we wander the chaos from morning till night.
With laughter our compass, we roam absurd lanes,
In a world full of wonders, not meant to be tamed.

Unwritten Chapters in the Soul

A book left unopened collects quite a dust,
Filled with blank pages, yet rich with our trust.
The ink never flows, but stories still tease,
In the silence of laughter, we find our unease.

With socks that don't match and hair that won't stay,
We scribble our tales in a quirky ballet.
Like children with crayons on walls made of sin,
Each scribble a chapter that sparks from within.

The fridge is a canvas; the magnets dance bold,
With "what's for dinner?" — a mystery untold.
Pickles on cupcakes, a culinary craze,
In the cookbook of nonsense, we find our own ways.

So here's to the moments that we can't explain,
The joy in our stumbles, the chuckles in pain.
For pages unwritten are treasures to hold,
In the chapters of spirit that never grow old.

The Weight of Invisible Anchors

We float down the street, like balloons on a whim,
Carrying burdens that always feel grim.
The anchor of laundry, it drags us along,
As we belt out our lives in a comical song.

With coffee as armor, we march into tasks,
While wearing a smile, in disguise we bask.
The dreams that we carry like hats on our heads,
Become tangled with wishes, and oh, they're a spread!

Our worries are whispers, they tell us to frown,
Yet we choose to laugh as we tumble around.
With socks on the ceiling and pencils in hair,
In the circus of chaos, we dance with a flair.

So we'll pack up our anchors, and float with the breeze,
In the ocean of nonsense, we do as we please.
For laughter's our lifeboat, we sail with delight,
In a world full of madness, we're ready for flight!

Silhouettes of Collective Memory

In the back of the bus, echoes of cheers,
We share tales of ketchup and childhood fears.
With crayons that melted on sunny hot days,
Nostalgia's a game with a million ways.

A friend once asked 'Why is your shoe on a cat?'
We laughed 'til we cried, what a curious spat.
The pages of history, splattered in fun,
Rewind and repeat, oh, where have we run?

Our memories flicker like lights in the dark,
While shadows of laughter go chasing a spark.
With jokes that we borrowed from comedians old,
In this gallery of giggles, our stories unfold.

So let's toast to the moments that dance through the years,
To the silliness woven in smiles, not tears.
In the silhouettes painted on walls of our heart,
Each chuckle a treasure, a hilariously art!

The Journey Through Shadows

In the quest for wisdom, we roam,
Dodging questions like a rolling gnome.
With every step, we trip and fall,
A grand circus, we laugh through it all.

We chase the stars, but miss the moon,
Expecting answers to come too soon.
Like searching for socks in a drying spin,
We find our joys where the chaos begins.

With each bright laugh, we shift and sway,
Finding delight in the muddled display.
Twists and turns, like a playful game,
The punchline never varies, but that's just our aim.

So here we wander, our heads held high,
With goofy grins as the questions fly.
In the shadowy dance of whims and dreams,
We're the jesters, or so it seems.

Canvas of Uncertain Colors

Brush in hand, we paint the scene,
A splash of blue on grass so green.
With every stroke, we'll splash and mix,
A masterpiece born from artistic tricks.

Colors collide without a plan,
A polka-dotted cat, a purple man.
Each hue a laugh, each blend a cheer,
In this joyful mess, we've nothing to fear.

Trying to find the right shade, we splatter,
Dodging the logic, what does it matter?
In the quirky swirls, we may just find,
A tapestry made of a colorful mind.

So grab your pigments, let's sing and play,
In this art of chaos, we'll find our way.
With brushes in hand, we'll chase the light,
And through each giggle, we paint our flight.

Threads of a Fragile Fabric

A tapestry woven with mismatched thread,
A game of stitching, we forge ahead.
With every knot, a chuckle unfolds,
In the fabric of life, it's laughter that holds.

Measuring wisdom with a crooked ruler,
The tailor of fate, a comical fooler.
Each patch a story, each seam a jest,
In this quilt of confusion, we're truly blessed.

From frayed edges to colors so bright,
We dance through the chaos, hearts full of light.
Stitches of joy, woven tight as can be,
In this bumpy ride, take a stitch with me.

As threads twist and tangle, we giggle and weave,
Crafting our saga, something to believe.
In the quirks of the fabric, we find our cheer,
A splendid patchwork of laughter we steer.

Treading Water in the Unknown

We're splashing around in a sea of doubt,
Making waves where the calm's about.
Wading through puddles, we float and glide,
With a rubber duck, we take it in stride.

Counting the fish as they swim on by,
Each fin a riddle, each tail a sigh.
In this deep end, we're flailing with glee,
Who knew that confusion could be so free?

The lifeguard yawns as we laugh and drift,
Juggling our worries, oh what a gift!
With buoyant hearts, we'll tread and twirl,
In this wobbly dance, we'll give it a whirl.

So let the waves come, we'll float along,
With goofy grins, we'll sing our song.
In the watery depths of the unknown,
We find our treasure, laughter is grown.

Unfolding in Different Directions

Like origami birds that flop,
We twist and turn with every drop.
Plans set firm like jelly rolls,
Who knew we'd take such silly strolls?

A map in hand, but where's the clue?
We dance in circles, just me and you.
Each signpost points another way,
They'd laugh at us, if they could stay.

Expectations high like a birthday cake,
Slicing through the layers, oh what a mistake!
Cream and sprinkles go flying wide,
Guess we're just along for the ride.

So here we are, a happy mess,
Finding joy in the quirky stress.
With every turn, a brand new spark,
Adventure waits in the vast unknown dark.

The Weight of Unspoken Words

Words piled high like laundry loads,
Each one a thought that silently goads.
We sigh and nod, but oh, so shy,
What would they say if we said hi?

Conversations full of awkward blinks,
Over cups of coffee and fruity drinks.
They say less is often more,
But what if less is just a bore?

Our brains like melting ice cream scoops,
So many thoughts, yet it's just us two groups.
Puns and laughter hang in the air,
Finding meaning just feels so rare.

Each smile we share, a heavy stone,
Carrying jokes we've never known.
But in this dance of silent glee,
What's unspoken's often meant to be.

Questions that Float Like Leaves

Questions drift like leaves in fall,
Spinning, whirling, sometimes a brawl.
What's next, they ask, with cheeky grins,
While we just laugh at where we've been.

Why's the sky blue and grass so green?
Curiosity hides in space between.
Unlocking mysteries with silly strife,
Holding onto threads of this quirky life.

Do ducks quack in a vast conundrum?
Or maybe they think life's just a humdrum?
Floating worries, like clouds they roam,
While we ponder where to call home.

So we ask, and we giggle too,
As questions sail in bizarre hues.
Each leaf that falls adds to the quilt,
Of all the fun we've ever built.

Between the Lines of a Forgotten Song

A tune once danced on the tips of tongues,
Now whispers faint, like forgotten young.
Notes like breadcrumbs scattered wide,
Hints of laughter in the glide.

The rhythm's lost, but hey, that's fine,
We'll make up verses with our own design.
We hop and skip; we twist and sway,
Creating new tunes in our own way.

Lyrics fade, but smiles stay bright,
Who needs a chorus when hearts take flight?
With silly tunes echoing around,
Joyful noise is what we've found.

So hum along, forget the rest,
Life's too short for a seriousness test.
Between the lines where laughter sings,
Is where the heart finds all its wings.

When Questions Outnumber Answers

Why do socks always disappear?
Are they seeking a new frontier?
I ponder as I search the floor,
For a pair, I can't ignore.

Why do we trip on our own feet?
Is gravity playing a trick? How neat!
I laugh as I do my dance,
With each stumble, I take a chance.

What's the reason for all this fuss?
Do we really need to discuss?
Unraveled thoughts fly here and there,
Like a cat just caught the air.

Is this a riddle or a jest?
Maybe jesters know the best.
I'll wear my shoes, with or without,
And dance on with a merry shout.

Searching for Stars in Daylight

I look for stars in morning's glow,
But the sun steals the cosmic show.
Where'd they go, those twinkling sprites?
Maybe they're just on Netflix nights.

The sky is blue, so wide and grand,
Yet the stars must've made a plan.
Maybe they're at an intergalactic bar,
Sipping juice from a candy jar.

Am I the only one who's lost?
Looking for wonders at any cost?
Daylight hides what nighttime shares,
So, I'll chase the sun in my old pairs.

With shades on eyes and a smile wide,
I stroll with dreams, a goofy stride.
For fun arrives no matter the hour,
Even if stars hide like blooming flowers.

The Fragrance of Impermanent Moments

Like fresh cookies, they come and go,
Sweet smells whisk away in flow.
Just like laughter, a burst so brief,
It's in those giggles we find relief.

The breeze carries whispers of joy,
Was it a puppy? Or just a toy?
Ephemeral scents ride on the air,
Tickling noses, a moment to spare.

Like a balloon that pops so fast,
Memories linger, but they don't last.
I chase after thoughts, oh what a race,
Looking for comfort in time and space.

Yet every hiccup, grin, or sigh,
Is a sprinkle of humor that won't die.
I'll soak in the scents, now and then,
For impermanence is a party with friends.

In the Silence of the Unspoken

In quiet corners, laughter hides,
With silly jokes that humor rides.
Why's the chicken across the street?
To avoid my two-left shoes on fleet!

Silent giggles fill the room,
While puns dance, dispelling gloom.
What's unsaid hangs thick in air,
Like spaghetti caught in wild hair.

A wink exchanged, a sly tease,
Leaves us doubled over, at ease.
Words may fail, but smiles obey,
In the comical chaos of the day.

So here we sit, with unshared wit,
Finding joy in every little bit.
In silence, we echo and compose,
A symphony where humor grows.

Fleeting Threads of Existence

In a world where socks disappear,
I ponder my purpose, loud and clear.
Like Friday's pizza, cheesy and bright,
I seek a reason in the late-night light.

The cat chases shadows, quite absurd,
While I try to catch the thought I heard.
Balloons float high, some just won't land,
Is there a secret I don't understand?

The clock ticks slow, like molasses run,
Is tomorrow's joke already begun?
I trip on wisdom, oh so profound,
But wisdom's got jokes, most are just sound.

And when I wake up, what will I see?
Just another Tuesday wondering 'me'.
Perhaps the answer's in breakfast toast,
Or the socks that I lost, they matter the most!

When Purpose Hides

I looked for meaning in the garden's weeds,
Found only rabbits munching on seeds.
Chasing my shadow as it runs away,
This game of hide-and-seek, come what may.

The toaster's singing, but bread's in denial,
Where are my plans? They're lost in a pile.
Like a duck in the rain, I splashed and clucked,
While pondering puzzles, I'm so unstuck.

Jelly spills like secrets on my shirt,
Mismatched socks are life's little flirt.
Is the meaning hidden in the dessert?
Or is it just crumbs, got me feeling inert?

I ponder and muse, like a wise old sage,
As a fly lands on my book, quite the page.
It buzzes and dances, knows more than I,
Perhaps I should simply take to the sky!

The Silence of Unraveled Thoughts

My thoughts are tangled like yarn on the floor,
Each one I unravel leads to four more.
They laugh at me softly, 'No end in sight,'
Even my coffee's gone cold, what a plight.

The hamster wheel spins, but it won't get far,
I'm chasing my goals wrapped up in a jar.
With jelly beans dancing, and giggles around,
I wonder if silence makes much of a sound.

A sock puppet whispers, 'Is here the right place?'
While I search for answers in soft, furry grace.
The universe chuckles, a cosmic prank,
Dropping truth bombs in a kid's piggy bank.

But wait, what's this? A spark in the mind—
Maybe there's joy in the chaos I find.
So I'll tie the loose ends and dance with a cheer,
For nonsense is wisdom, let's guffaw here!

Where Dreams Drift Aimlessly

A boat made of wishes floats past where I stand,
With dreams as its sails, not quite as planned.
The oars are mischief, row left then row right,
Heading to nowhere under stars that invite.

The compass spins wildly with laughter and glee,
Nautical nonsense, just come sail with me!
A fish swims by, wearing a top hat,
And I forget my worries, how about that?

If goals are like jellybeans, scattered around,
I'll scoop them all up from the pink, and the brown.
One's got a secret, or so I have heard,
With a nibble of wisdom, a giggle, a word.

So here's to the drifting, the whims of the tide,
Where meaning's a riddle that we wear with pride.
In the sea of the silly, I'll float and I'll dream,
Finding joy in the journey, flowing with the stream!

The Weight of Unasked Questions

Why did the chicken cross the road?
To ponder the question she once owed.
With every step, she lost her thought,
Like socks in the dryer, she came to naught.

A squirrel asked why the sky was blue,
But all he got was a funny view.
As bees buzzed by without a care,
He shrugged it off, a nutty affair.

The cat looked wise with its sly little grin,
Yet pondered the catch, where to begin?
Should one ask why pancakes stack so high?
Or just eat them warm and let out a sigh?

So here we sit, a head full of fluff,
Debating the meaning of all this stuff.
Embrace the jest, don't squint your eyes,
For questions unasked are the funniest lies.

Caught Between Dreams and Reality

In a dream, I found a swimming pool,
Filled with popcorn, now that's the rule!
I dove right in, it felt so grand,
Until I woke up, with butter on my hand.

The moon whispered secrets, oh what a tease,
While I tried to convince it to be my cheese.
But dreams tend to slip like soap in a shower,
And I woke up late, feeling less than dower.

There's a fine line 'tween wish and want,
Like being chased by a giant daunt.
I ran through the fields of my silly thoughts,
Only to realize I forgot my socks.

So here's to the worlds that twist and bend,
Where the absurd is common, and dreams pretend.
We laugh at the chaos that fills our nights,
Cuz reality hits, but it's fun to take flights!

The Illusion of Knowing

I thought I knew how to bake a cake,
But it turned out to be a big mistake.
Flour in my hair and eggs on the floor,
I guess Googling "easy" was quite a bore!

My neighbor claims he's seen the stars,
Yet I caught him stargazing at passing cars.
With a telescope made of tin cans and tape,
He swears he can find the right shape!

The expert said, "Just trust the signs,"
While tripping over his own punchlines.
So here's to wisdom that often misleads,
Like planting a garden with candy seeds.

In the end, we laugh with chips on our shoulders,
Because knowing so much just makes us bolder.
Embrace the absurdity and don't be shy,
For what we think we know is a comical lie!

Beneath the Surface of Time

Tick-tock, tick-tock, what does it mean?
A race against seconds, so often unseen.
I paused for a snack, left time in my wake,
And realized I'm just one big mistake!

My calendar's filled with to-dos galore,
Yet I can't find my keys, oh what a chore!
The clock keeps on ticking, it seems so cruel,
As I run in circles like a dizzy fool.

"How old are you?" is a question so fraught,
I answer with cake, like it matters a lot.
For beneath every candle, there lies a fun truth,
We're all just big kids pretending our youth.

So let's dance with the time, in a wacky parade,
And laugh as we find all the moments we've made.
Because the surface may shimmer, but underneath shine,
Are the priceless missteps that make life divine.

Riddles in the Rain

Puddles splash, shoes squeak loud,
Umbrellas turned inside-out,
What is wet and loves to joke?
A sky so gray, it can't figure out.

Raindrops dance, a wobbly beat,
Chasing clouds on a whim's retreat,
Each drop whispers secrets anew,
But can a raindrop keep its cue?

Laughter lingers, echoing wide,
As thunder rolls, a stormy ride,
We jump in puddles, dreams afloat,
Finding joy in our chance remote.

So skip through showers, grin so bright,
Who cares if the sun's out of sight?
For every riddle the rain can spin,
A giggle hides where joy begins.

The Dance of Uncertainty

Two left feet, a clumsy sway,
The dance begins in disarray,
With moonlit steps that twist and turn,
While partners stumble, awkwardly learn.

The music skips, a note confined,
Are we lost or just unkind?
As every twirl leads to confusion,
We laugh at our own delusion.

Fingers point, the critics stare,
But who needs grace when laughs are rare?
A spin, a leap, all wildly bold,
In our crazy waltz, true tales unfold.

So dance, my friend, with no regret,
For even mishaps can be a duet;
With every misstep, joy we'll find,
In this quirky dance of the carefree mind.

Reflections in a Broken Mirror

A cracked glass laughs at my surprise,
Sixteen faces with silly eyes,
Who's the fairest of them all?
I can't tell with this wild brawl.

One side grins while the other frowns,
Jokes abound in my town of clowns,
Each shard holds secrets, half-formed tales,
Of awkward moments and shoe fails.

I check my hair, a tangled spree,
How does this happen? Can't I see?
The mirror plays its cheeky game,
Who knew looking close could feel so lame?

So here I stand, in fractured view,
Laughing at all I thought I knew;
In pieces lies my truest face,
A puzzle where I find my place.

Beneath the Weight of Stars

Stars above, they blink and tease,
A cosmic joke on a gentle breeze,
Why so far? What's the big show?
Twinkling secrets, do they even know?

Constellations whisper tales of old,
In shimmering lights, their stories unfold,
But counting each star is quite a task,
Is there a reason? No one will ask.

So here we lay with our dreams so bright,
Pinching ourselves to check if it's night;
For every wish upon a light,
Is just our way to dance with delight.

So lift your gaze, why not partake?
In the weight of stars, there's laughter to make;
For in the universe, vast and grand,
We find our humor, hand in hand.

The Uncharted Waters of Being

I set sail on my tiny boat,
With a sardine for bait and hope to float.
The map's all smudged, the compass spins,
I wave to dolphins who surely have wins.

I chart my course with a rubber duck,
In stormy seas, I say, "What the pluck?"
To find the treasure lost long ago,
Is it wisdom or just a soggy shoe?

I fish for answers in a mud puddle,
Catch a memory—a funny little cuddle.
But every wave just tosses me round,
As I wonder how I got here, not a clue to be found.

So I paddle on, don't know where I'll be,
With a sandwich and pickle, just me and my sea.
Though I'm lost at sea, I just laugh and sing,
For what's more fun than not knowing a thing!

Threads that Tangle and Unravel

I knitted a sweater with yarn from a cat,
Look, it's a scarf! Or is it a hat?
The pattern was clear, but I lost my way,
Now it's a blanket where I wish I could stay.

My grandma warned me, "Be careful, dear!"
But I was too busy trying new gear.
With needles that danced, I tried to entwine,
A potpourri of chaos, a grand design!

Each stitch I made was a puzzle to solve,
A jumbled creation that won't quite evolve.
As I pulled on the yarn, it started to squeal,
And I realized my sweater was not so ideal.

Yet here I sit, in my tangle of thread,
With patterns unheard and colors widespread.
It might look a mess, but it's cozy and warm,
In this knitted enigma, I find comfort, not alarm!

When Clarity Fades

I woke up today with a plan in my head,
But it vanished like toast that I burnt instead.
The sunshine was bright, the sky looked so blue,
Then I tripped on my thoughts—did I forget my shoe?

I scribbled a list, it had a few jots,
But the ink ran away, left me with knots.
I asked my goldfish; he just stared with glee,
While he swam in circles not helping me see.

The clock keeps on ticking, yet time stands so still,
I tried to find sense, but I'm out of goodwill.
With a wink and a shrug, I decide to embrace,
This delightful confusion, this chaotic space.

So I dance with my doubts, a quirky old tune,
Life's a bizarre circus, under a patchy moon.
When clarity fades, I still find the fun,
In the art of dodging decisions, I run!

The Color of Uncertainty

I picked up my crayons, thought I'd create,
A picture of wisdom—oh, what a fate!
But the colors just blended, became a big smear,
Now it's a canvas that provokes a lost tear.

The blue turned to green; the red cried for pink,
Each stroke of my hand made me rethink.
So I splashed some confetti on my canvas of doubt,
And chuckled, 'What's art if you can't twist it about?'

With a splash of confusion and a dash of flair,
My masterpiece grows into a jumbled affair.
If life is a drawing that doesn't make sense,
I'll turn it to laughter; that's my recompense!

So bring on the chaos, the smears and the stains,
In this wacky wide world, I'll dance in the rains.
For the color of uncertainty is bright like a fire,
I've learned to find joy in the unexpected mire!

The Gentle Chaos of Existence

In a world where ducks wear shoes,
I search for signs, but find just clues.
A sandwich talks, a cat does dance,
   Existence plays its silly prance.

I trip on wisdom dressed in hats,
Chasing thoughts that run like cats.
The sun throws shade, the moon throws light,
   While squirrels plot to steal a bite.

I ask a tree, what's with the bark?
It whispers jokes that hit the mark.
A tumbleweed rolls by so slow,
   Reminds me I can also flow.

So here's to chaos, beer, and cheese,
A life that's lived with goofy ease.
In every twist, a laugh will ring,
In gentle chaos, we find our spring.

Navigating the Ocean of Ambiguity

A fish in a hat is quite absurd,
Yet he swears he's never heard,
Of maps or stars that guide our way,
He prefers to just swim and play.

Sailing on thoughts of jellybeans,
We drift through waves of silly scenes.
The ocean's vast, but humor flows,
Where confusion blooms, and logic slows.

With each wave crashing on the shore,
We toss our troubles, leave them poor.
A rubber duck floats by my side,
Together we laugh, our fears collide.

Navigating life with noodle boats,
In strange waters where laughter floats.
Of meaning lost, or so they say,
I'll take the fun in every sway.

Sifting Through Moments of Stillness

In silence, I hear a guitar weep,
While shadows gather, secrets keep.
A cactus giggles, pricks its toes,
In quiet times, absurdity grows.

I sit with time, a slice of pie,
And ponder why the pancakes fly.
A ghostly sheep counts over me,
Making stillness feel like a spree.

Moments linger like old cheese scent,
Wrapping me in a laugh intent.
The clock ticks slow, yet I run fast,
In stillness found, a joy amassed.

So here's to pauses, giggles and grins,
Where wisdom wears mismatched shoes and fins.
In every moment, crisp and clear,
Absurdity makes the meaning steer.

Beyond the Limits of Understanding

In a land where socks go to hide,
I searched for answers with a wide-eyed glide.
The fridge hums secrets in its cool embrace,
Yet the butter just laughs, keeping its place.

The cat claims wisdom in every nap,
While I ponder the meaning of the dust on the map.
With each cup of coffee, my thoughts fly around,
But answers still hide, where they can't be found.

Veils of Enigma

A riddle wrapped in a soft taco shell,
A donut that whispers, "All is swell!"
I chased a rainbow on a Tuesday morn,
And discovered it led me to a unicorn's horn.

The fish in the bowl, they gaze and they stare,
Asking the questions I cannot bear.
Why do I trip over my own two feet?
Answers wander off like they're hard to greet.

The Silence Between Heartbeats

Between two thoughts, a pesky squirrel waits,
Counting acorns while dodging my fate.
The crossword puzzle holds no clear clue,
As I scribble nonsense in powder blue.

Between the heartbeats, the silence hums,
Like a thousand bees with their tiny drums.
I laugh at the chaos, I dance in the dark,
While searching for meaning in a stray dog's bark.

Light Breaking Through the Fog

Through the fog, I see the sun on a stick,
It winked at my glasses, which cracked with a flick.
A snail on a quest for the fastest race,
Drags his shell while dreaming of outer space.

The toaster pops up a slice of surprise,
A breakfast dance under morning skies.
Light might break through, but the coffee is cold,
Still, I chuckle through days both dull and bold.

Glimmers of a Distant Light

A chicken crossed the street one day,
To find out just what folks would say.
Was it for love or just for the show?
Now guess if she even knows where to go!

The stars above wink in delight,
As we fumble through days and nights.
Searching for answers in a cereal box,
Who knew wisdom comes from frosted flocks?

We dance in the rain, we trip on our feet,
Laughing at puddles, oh what a treat!
The universe chuckles, a cosmic jest,
While we wear mismatched socks with zest.

So raise a toast to all things absurd,
To straying paths we've rarely heard.
For every misstep leads to a grin,
Perhaps that's where we truly begin!

A Canvas of Unwritten Stories

A painter's brush with colors so bright,
Swirled random thoughts in the morning light.
Yet when asked the purpose, she shrugs and grins,
Art doesn't need meaning—just splatters and spins!

There's a cat in a hat who sips on tea,
Wonders aloud, what's a 'me' without 'we'?
As he ponders deeply, he spills all his brew,
And laughs while he thinks, 'What next to pursue?'

The clock ticks softly with an echoing thud,
Tickling our minds like a giggling bud.
What's an hour when lost in a thought?
Maybe it's time for a snack that we've sought!

In the end, we scribble with crayons and glee,
Confusing the fates with our playful decree.
Each stroke tells a story, a sweet little lie,
And we ponder the question—oh my, oh my!

The Tide of Forgotten Realities

Once upon a dream, a fish learned to sing,
With a tune that could make the forest swing.
But every time he tried to take flight,
He flopped and flailed, what a silly sight!

Waves come crashing like laughter at play,
Making sandcastles that wash away.
Why build them high when they won't last long?
Maybe they know where they truly belong!

Seashells are whispers from cultures gone by,
They tell tales of laughter, and sometimes a sigh.
But who's to recall what the ocean once said?
Perhaps it recalled sleeping sharks' bedtime spread.

So let's wade through the nonsense like children at sea,
With buckets of joy, let the tide set us free.
For in waves of chaos, there's buoyancy felt,
Every splash a wonder, every laugh heartfelt!

Whispers of the Unfathomable

A sock lost its partner, what a bold claim!
It declares independence, what a wild game!
Floats in a laundry basket full of surprise,
Whispers of freedom, oh how it flies!

The moon in the night plays peek-a-boo bright,
While the stars giggle softly at the curious plight.
What's the meaning behind this grand dance?
Maybe it's just a cosmic romance!

The toaster pops out a mystical glow,
Much like our thoughts that ebb and flow.
Conveniently burnt, yet remarkably cheery,
Warm crusty humor, never too dreary!

So gather your wits, let the quirks play their part,
In this absurdity, we'll find a new art.
Forget all the questions that nag at the core,
And enjoy this bizarre encore once more!

The Search for Shadows

I looked for shadows in the sun,
But all I found was a rubber bun.
It bounced around like a lost balloon,
Telling jokes to a friendly raccoon.

I asked the sun where shadows go,
He hummed a tune, then said, "No show!"
Just then, a squirrel with a floppy hat,
Said, "Hey buddy, why care about that?"

In the Midst of the Clouds

I sat on clouds and sipped my tea,
While raindrops danced just out of reach.
They whispered secrets, oh so sly,
About the cows who wished to fly.

A rainbow giggled, bright and bold,
Telling tales of the sky's gold.
I chased it down, but it slipped away,
As birds sang songs of yesterday.

Whispers Between the Pages

In a book, I met a wise old snail,
Who claimed to have the secret trail.
He pulled out maps of spaghetti roads,
While I scratched my head and juggled toads.

The pages rustled with a cheeky grin,
Teasing thoughts, I'm lost again!
Yet every word felt like a feast,
With laughter ringing, at least to me, at least.

Echoes of an Unanswered Question

I pondered on a question so deep,
Why do socks vanish? They never creep.
In cupboards dark, they play a game,
Leaving me to clutch my last pair in shame.

The echoes laughed, they found it funny,
As I searched for one, it felt like a punny.
I threw my hands up in sheer delight,
And danced with the laundry, what a sight!

The Beauty of Life's Transitions

Sometimes I trip on my own shoes,
Like a clown without a clue.
The road ahead is filled with bends,
But laughter is where the journey ends.

Each turn reveals a brand new scene,
Like a movie not yet seen.
With every slip, a chance to dance,
And wardrobe malfunctions make us prance.

A sandwich falls, jelly side down,
I wear it like a messy crown.
The universe plays a funny game,
With punchlines that are never the same.

So grab a snack and take a ride,
On this rollercoaster side by side.
Through highs and lows, we'll laugh and cheer,
In this comedy, we hold so dear.

Searching for Balance in Chaos

Juggling snacks while walking straight,
Is this skill or just my fate?
The world spins like a top so fast,
I'm dizzy now, can't think, alas!

Coffee spills while counting sheep,
Work-life balance? Never sleep!
Emails ding, and phones all buzz,
I'm lost in this chaotic fuzz.

Yet in the midst of all this mess,
I find sweet joy in the distress.
A smirk, a wink, a funny glance,
Life's too wild; let's take a chance!

When storms arise, I might just dance,
Spinning circles, I take my stance.
With laughter as my saving grace,
In chaos, I find my place.

The Echo of Untold Stories

Behind the curtain, whispers grow,
Of silly tales and truths we know.
An echo bounces, laughs resound,
With every secret, joy is found.

A cat on a roof with quite a view,
Might think it's a king, but who knew?
A sandwich tossed, a dog in flight,
These stories bloom in day and night.

From missed trains to socks that don't match,
Each funny moment is a perfect catch.
We write our scripts with goofy pens,
And turn our fumbles into wins.

So gather 'round, let tales unfold,
With laughter as our greatest gold.
In every chuckle, in every cheer,
Life's a story, so hold it near.

Shadows Passing Through

Shadows dance in the bright sunlight,
Creating shapes that feel just right.
Like behind the lens of a quirky show,
Where nothing's perfect, but fun can grow.

A shadow of a squirrel, bold and spry,
Dancing like it's trying to fly.
Each silhouette tells some odd tale,
Of mishaps and laughter that never fail.

In a world where shadows often blend,
We find humor around each bend.
So let them pass, those darkened views,
For joy will come with brightening hues.

It's not the shadows that matter most,
But the laughter we share, that we can boast.
Let's lighten the mood, and take a step,
In the dance of shadows, we choose to rep.

Searching for Light in the Abyss

In the depths I roam, so deep,
Chasing shadows that never leap.
With a flashlight that flickers and pops,
I trip on my thoughts as the chaos hops.

I ask the stars if they've seen my way,
They wink at me, then choose to sway.
The abyss laughs with its echoing sound,
I dance with the darkness, all logic unbound.

But who knew the void came with such flair?
It's a cosmic giggle, a dark carnival air.
I might not find answers, oh what a bummer,
Yet I'm laughing and tumbling, what a delightful blunder!

So here in the gloom where wisdom can't gleam,
I sip on confusion, life's illogical dream.
With a grin on my face, I embrace the unknown,
For in this grand folly, I've truly grown.

The Puzzle with Missing Pieces

Sat on the floor with a big puzzle box,
One piece is missing, now I'm in a flux.
Flip it and twist it, a mystery to solve,
Turns out my brain's in a dizzy dissolve.

The cat thinks it's fun, she sits on the mat,
While I pull at my hair and shout, 'Where's that flat?'
Every corner I check, yet none seem to fit,
Maybe it's hiding, just playing a skit.

I wonder if puzzles even need all their parts,
Would it matter if life's art had missing charts?
Could a missing edge just give it some flair?
A masterpiece formed in the chaos we share.

So I laugh at the pieces spread all around,
The jumble of colors is life's circus sound.
Incomplete but enchanted, it's quite a sweet mess,
These flaws in my puzzle? They'll lead to finesse.

A Journey on Worn-Out Paths

With worn-out shoes on this bumpy route,
I take one step forward, and then I scoot.
The path twists and turns like a wobbly funk,
But wow, what a ride in this jiggly junk!

Each pebble I trip on gives me a story,
To tell at the end while basking in glory.
I laugh with the squirrels, they offer advice,
"Just go with the wobble, it'll feel nice!"

The compass is broken, the map's upside-down,
Every dead end feels like a festive clown.
But joy fills the air as I skip on my way,
These missteps are gems that brighten my day.

So here's to the paths that don't lead to score,
I'll dance with the chaos; who could want more?
Each wrinkled road whispers loudly and clear,
That wandering off course is the best part, my dear.

Fragments of a Fading Dawn

The morning sun peeks, a shy little sprite,
Painting the clouds in colors so bright.
Yet my coffee's cold, the toast burnt to black,
I'm ruminating on dreams like a silly quack.

With winks from the sky that seem all too frail,
I chase after shadows that flicker and pale.
"What's the point?" I sip, in a pondering swirl,
As the dawn throws glitter, a chaotic whirl.

I hear whispers of meaning, but they giggle and fade,
Like the crumbs from my breakfast, all scattered and played.
Yet I'm waving goodbye to the whispered dark fears,
With a wink of my own and a laugh through the tears.

So hold on to fragments of moments so kind,
Even if logic seems purposely blind.
I'll ride the day's whimsy, embrace every flaw,
For in this sweet chaos, I'll find my own law.

In the Forest of Misconceptions

In the forest where trees talk back,
Squirrels argue, thoughts go off track.
The path is twisted, a curious ride,
Who knew that acorns could gossip and bide?

Badger wears glasses, claims he's profound,
While hedgehogs debate what's lost and found.
The owl hoots mysteries, all for a laugh,
But no one's got answers—just a silly half!

Fox plays the flute, a jazzy delight,
But raccoons prefer a moonlit fight.
In this confusion, fun finds its way,
Who needs clarity when you can play?

So wander the woods, where nonsense is king,
Cherish the quirks that this forest can bring.
For meaning? Who cares? Just follow the fun,
In a tangle of laughter, our hearts can run!

Burdens of Unanswered Whys

Questions hang heavy like clouds in the sky,
Why do ducks quack, and the kittens just sigh?
The gravity of wonder pulls everyone flat,
As turtles ponder why they're never a hat.

A goat in the meadow, with a sage-like frown,
Asks why humans wear those silly crowns.
But who has the time for those deep, endless sighs?
When llamas in tutus just dance in reprise.

Stray cats in sunglasses lounge on the wall,
They know their life's purpose is simply to sprawl.
Meanwhile, ants gear up for a complex debate,
On whether the crumb can await or just wait.

So toss your big whys in the great, wild breeze,
And dance with the answers (if any) that tease.
In this jolly mess, a giggle persists,
For curiosity wins when confusion exists!

The River of Uncertain Currents

Down the river where waves tickle toes,
Fish tell tall tales, or so everyone knows.
The rocks roll their eyes at the boat full of frogs,
While beavers build bridges they forget where they logs.

Here floats a rubber duck in a sailor's hat,
Trying to navigate, but he's got no map.
The current's uncertain, yet full of surprise,
As turtles surf waves, wearing casual ties.

A crab asks a shrimp if he's seen the way,
They just end up dancing—no need for convey.
The current of nonsense flows on and on,
With laughter and splashes from dusk until dawn.

So grab your adventures, embark on a float,
In the river of life, just enjoy the remote.
When purpose is wobbly, just paddle with cheer,
In these goofy waters, your smile will steer!

Serendipity in the Midst of Confusion

In the land where socks disappear at night,
A curious fairy makes mismatched delight.
Searching for wisdom, a hamster finds cheese,
While juggling his worries with whimsical ease.

A pineapple wearing a bowtie and shoes,
Claims that confusion is just fancy news.
While ants in a line host a grand parade,
Shouting, 'Find your rhythm!' in chaos displayed.

Pickles wear crowns on a cabbage throne,
Each vegetable chuckling, none feel alone.
And as folks trip over each jumbled thought,
The magic of nonsense is all that they've sought.

So dance with the weird, let the giggles commence,
In this quirky world, it just makes more sense.
For serendipity sparkles with joy in disguise,
In the muddle of life, see the wonder arise!

www.ingramcontent.com/pod-product-compliance
Lightning Source LLC
Chambersburg PA
CBHW051631160426
43209CB00004B/606